This is Billie
by Alice "Auntie Bubble" Lam

NAMA PRESS
Lockhart • Austin • New York

Nama Press
Lockhart and Austin, Texas & New York, New York

©2025 by Alice Lam

Library of Congress Cataloging-in-Publication Data

Lam, Alice, 1975 –
This is Billie / Alice Lam
ISBN: 979-8-9985583-0-6

First Edition

This is Billie.

She's my kitty.

We live together

in New York City.

Her eyes are big.

They're very round.

Her meow is like a squeaking sound.

Her fur is soft.

Her purr is loud.

She likes to go

where she's not allowed.

Her game of choice is basketball.

She runs like crazy down the hall.

She loves to climb

to high up places.

When I go out,

she unties my laces.

When I get home, this is her greeting.

She invites herself to online meetings.

At dinnertime,

she steals my food.

There are days

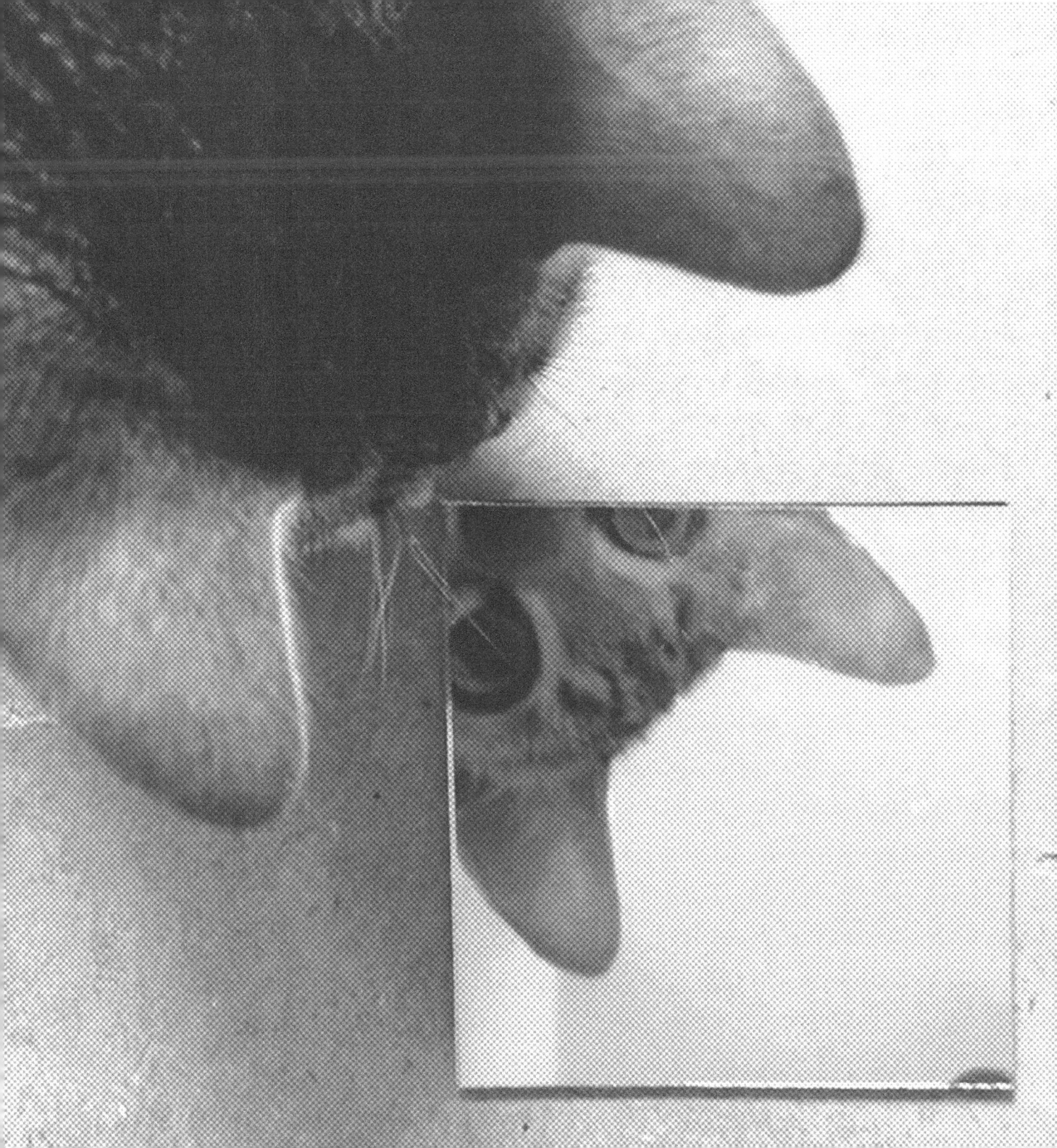

she's in a mood.

If she is bored,

she jumps
on my shoulder.

If she is tired,

**she insists
I hold her.**

When she does

what she should not,

it's kinda funny

when she gets caught.

Throughout it all,

I say to Billie...

as you grow up

please stay silly!

You can be grumpy.

You can be proud.

You can have

your head in the clouds.

Sure, we might have stressful days...

There'll be times I'm far away...

No matter what trouble

you might get into...

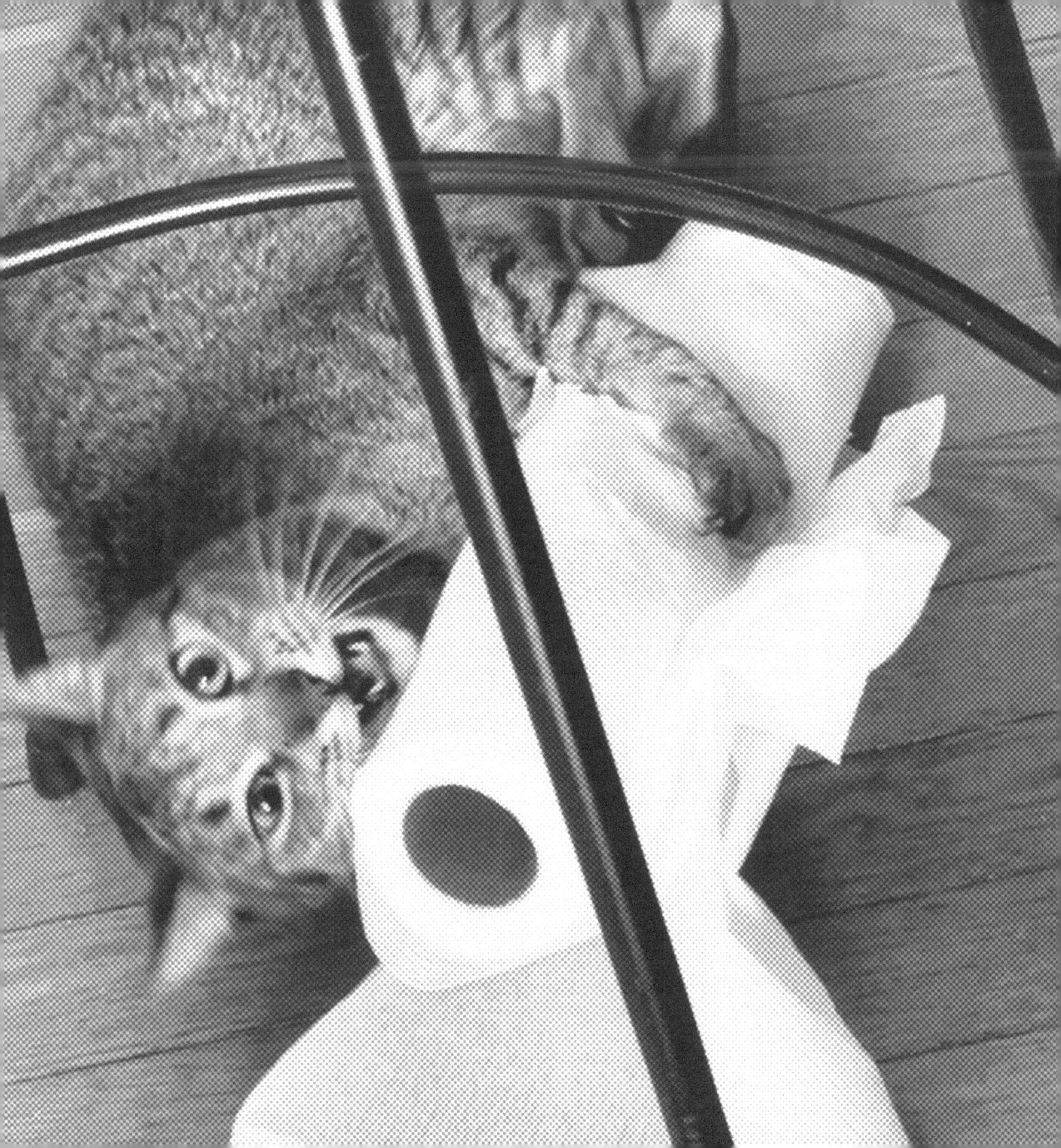

I will always

always

always

love you.

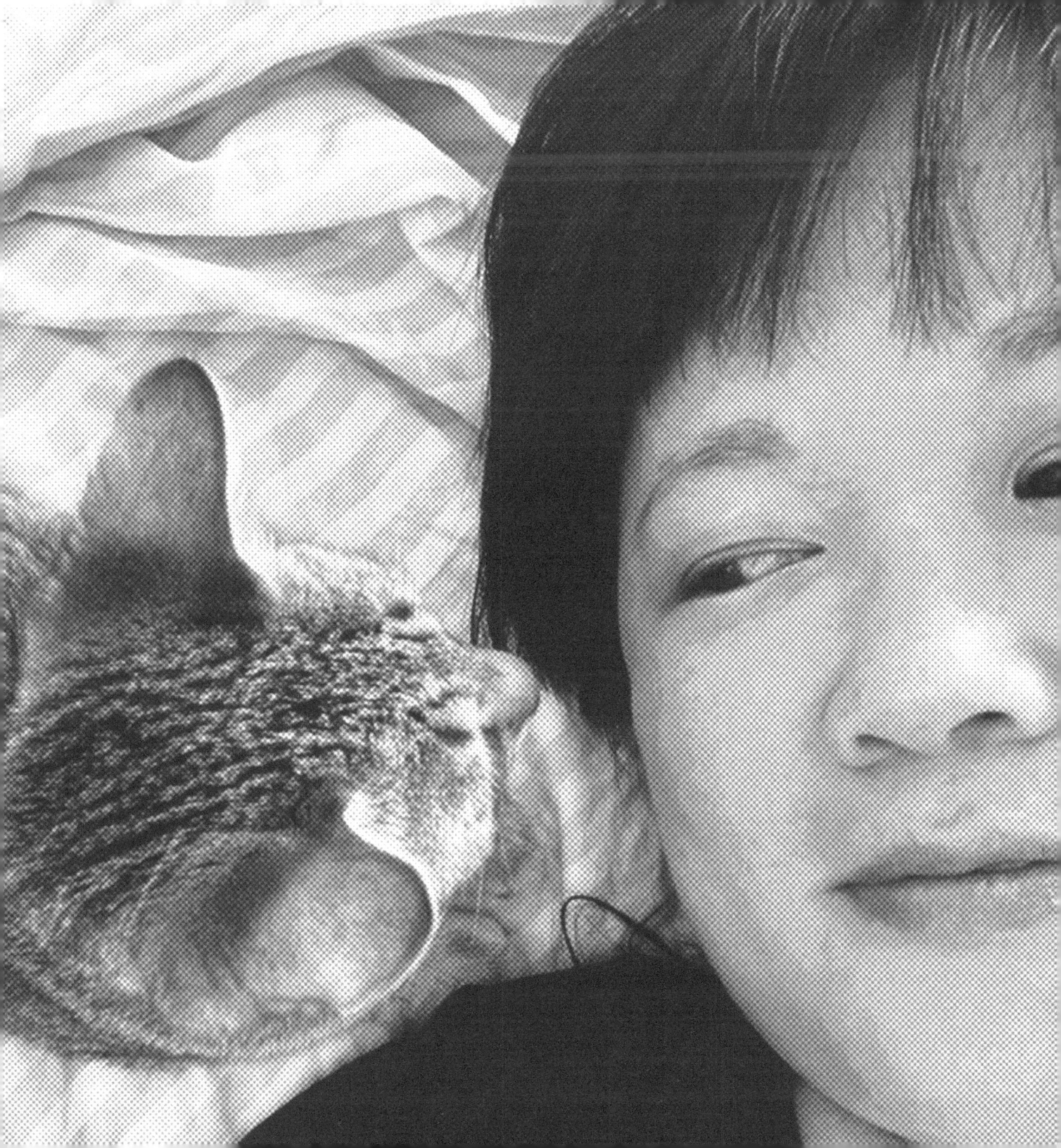

For Kaia
For Ellie
For Avelyn

♡,
Auntie
Bubble

www.ingramcontent.com/pod-product-compliance
Lightning Source LLC
Chambersburg PA
CBHW051326110526
44582CB00003B/59